Bir

City

EDITED BY
ANDY SAINT

CARLTON
BOOKS

First published by Carlton Books 2005

This book is not an officially licensed product of
Birmingham City Football Club

Text and design copyright © Carlton Books Limited 2005

A CIP catalogue record for this book is available
from the British Library.

ISBN 1 84442 462 6

Printed in Singapore

INTRODUCTION

How do you spell Birmingham City? P.O.T.E.N.T.I.A.L. No, they're NOT sleeping giants (giants are big and, in the full meaning of the word, Birmingham City have never quite been). Football's eternal bridesmaids they may be, but they're not hopeless… in fact, that's part of the trouble. Blues tease their fans with hints of being contenders, only to let them down time and again. Thus, their 130-year history is liberally sprinkled with great players, larger-than-life characters, famous victories, great cup runs and even a couple of rather good teams . Oh, and the biggest side terrace in English football, housing as intense and passionate a set of fans as you'll find, singing one of the all-time great club songs. Now, how do you spell Birmingham City? N.E.V.E.R. A. D.U.L.L. M.O.M.E.N.T.!

❝The fortunes of the club
are followed with keen interest
by the local residents in Small Heath.
The feeling of local pride that
was evinced in football clubs of
a few years ago is more completely
preserved in Small Heath
than elsewhere.**❞**

The Birmingham Gazette, January 1894

> **❛**The wild uncultured rushes of the forwards might be likened to the attacks of the Swazis or Zulus.**❜**

The Birmingham Mail describes Blues' somewhat physical performance against Sheffield Wednesday, 1900

‘We question whether [the club's] Directors are wise in pitching their camp in such unsavoury surroundings. ’

The Birmingham Mail expresses reservations at the club's plan to move to St Andrews, 1906

❝I completely forgot all about it.**❞**

Frank Richards, Secretary-Manager, on why
he failed to enter Blues for the FA Cup in the
1921–22 season

❝He played an absolute blinder.❞

Sunderland forward **Bobby Gurney** describes the performance of Harry Hibbs in the 1931 FA Cup semi-final

❝I was so excited when I learnt of Blues' interest in me that when I went back to the training session I lost concentration and went sliding off onto the gravel edge. When I met up with Blues officials later that day I had both my hands bandaged and found it hard to sign the contract.**❞**

Prolific Blues forward **Harold Bodle**, 1938, on his last day at Rotherham United

❝However long I watch football, I don't think it will be my lot to see a more fair and greater sportsman than "Good Old Joe". Win or lose, I think everyone hopes to see him play.❞

Letter from a Villa fan to the *Birmingham Daily Gazette* before the Blues' 1931 FA Cup Final appearance in praise of record scorer 'Gentleman' Joe Bradford who notched 267 goals for the club

❝ We would have settled for a 1–0 win before the game. That would have been enough for our £2 win bonus. **❞**

Alex Govan, scorer in the 9–1 victory
over Liverpool, 1954

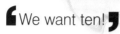

'We want ten!'

Blues fans get seriously greedy
versus Liverpool, 1954

❝Len Boyd was belting out "Any Old Iron" when the gaffer bellowed up the coach, "Let's have one from Scotland, Alex." I obliged with "Keep Right On To The End Of The Road". We sang it again and again until the entire coach was rocking as we pulled up outside Highbury. Blues fans picked up on the words and the rest is history.❞

Alex Govan remembers the birth of Blues' anthem in 1956

❝Birmingham City are the biggest favourites since the competition began.❞

The Birmingham Mail **FA Cup Final supplement**, 1956. Blues subsequently lost the final to Manchester City 3–1

❝We feel disappointed. We feel we have let you down.❞

Len Boyd, Blues skipper talking to 10,000 Blues fans at Snow Hill Station after arriving back from Wembley, 1956. 'No!,' roared the crowd in response to Boyd's comments

❝It was the biggest fluke in football I ever saw.❞

Roy Warhurst, describing Manchester City's winning goal in the FA Cup 6th Round, March 1958

❛I think that my days with Blues were the happiest part of my playing career.❜

Ken Leek, whose two goals clinched Blues' 3–1 League Cup Final win over Aston Villa in 1963

❛I rarely make forecasts but 16-year-old Bob Latchford will be really outstanding.**❜**

Manager **Stan Cullis**, 1967

❝When we were kicked by an opponent there was none of this squirming on the ground – we used to get back on our feet to show them we weren't hurt – even if we were. Trouble was, they'd kick us even harder next time just to make sure.❞

Cyril Trigg, Blues full-back, reminisces on a world of footballing hard men, BCFC programme, 1968

❝I think the lack of shin-guards proves that there is a lack of courage somewhere, or that tackles are not as hard as they used to be. Because if tackles were as full-blooded, it would need a man of Matthews' or Finney's ability to slip away unscathed.❞

Cyril Trigg

❛ Fairly skilful but needs speeding up. **❜**

The assessment of schoolboy **Trevor Francis** from Bisham Abbey, the national training centre, 1968

❝Francis 4 Bolton 0…**❞**

Sports Argus celebrates 16-year-old wonderboy
Trevor Francis's four-goal display against Bolton
Wanderers, February 20th 1971

❝ 1... 2... 3... 4... It's Francis! Trevor Francis shot himself into the record books when he mesmerised the Bolton Wanderers defence to become the first 16-year-old ever to score four goals in a Football League match. **❞**

Blues programme match report, 5th March 1971

‘Quite simply Trevor was the most remarkable youngster I have ever seen. He had so much ability and confidence in his ability but there was no arrogance about him, just supreme confidence in what he knew he could do. Even at 16 I had no doubts whatsoever that he would be a performer on the world stage.’

Bob Latchford talking about Trevor Francis

❛I've only seen him play once and I couldn't see what all the fuss was about. I much prefer to pack all my family off to the football on a Saturday afternoon and have a nice soak in the bath.**❜**

Mrs Iris Wright, Trevor Francis's landlady, BCFC match programme, February 1972

❝Football is my job and I just hope that I can get another role in the game when the time comes for me to retire as a player.**❞**

Former Blues winger **Gordon Taylor**, now Chairman of the PFA, November 1971

❝I don't care if it is a real bomb, I can go happy now I know that we're back in the First Division.**❞**

Sipping champagne, Chairman **Clifford Coombs** ignores police advice to evacuate Orient's Brisbane Road after Blues' 1–0 victory secured promotion, May 1972

❛I told everyone that, if necessary, we'd play until midnight to get the game finished❜

Referee **Edward Wallace** after pitch invasions and a bomb scare had delayed Blues' win at Orient

> **❛**I am sure the next decade will see great things happening in British soccer and that Birmingham City will be deeply involved in the events ahead.**❜**

Clifford Coombs, summer 1972

❛Birmingham City can be the team of the seventies. We want to win more than Leeds have, and we will because we are bolder.**❜**

Freddie Goodwin, Blues manager 1970–75,
May 1973

❝I'd rather the club go down
or I lose my job than sell any of
my best players.**❞**

Freddie Goodwin, *Birmingham Evening Mail*,
November 1973

❝This was the most difficult decision I have ever made in my managerial career.**❞**

Freddie Goodwin on the sale of Bob Latchford to Everton, *Birmingham Evening Mail*, February 1974

> **❝**It was a Pele goal, a Eusebio goal, a goal beyond the scope and dreams of most footballers.**❞**

The Birmingham Evening Mail's description of Trevor Francis's 35-yard wonder goal struck from near the touchline versus Carlisle United at St Andrews, March 25th 1975

❝Folk said they HAD seen sportsmen with such an intuitive sense of timing before. And then they used names like Sobers, Best and Law. A unique bond.❞

The Birmingham Evening Mail on the impact of
Trevor Francis's wonder goal against Carlisle
United at St Andrews, March 25th 1975

'Kenny Burns is like Willie Johnston or every other Jock with a claymore and Bannockburn in his blood. You either take him as you find him or you leave him alone.**'**

Birmingham Evening Mail, December 6th 1976

❛I think losing the 1975 FA Cup semi-final to Fulham set Birmingham City back twenty years.**❜**

Fan writing in the *125 Years of Birmingham City commemorative brochure*, 2000

❛The sale of Bob Latchford was not just the disposal of yet another home-produced asset – but the biggest kick in the teeth the club ever administered to its long-suffering fans. It rendered inevitable that the other three stars – Francis, Burns and Hatton – should depart as the club gave up any pretence of chasing serious honours.❜

Paul Baker, *...still journey on: The Birmingham City Story*, set for publication in 2006

❝I don't think it is fair that the fans should be tortured by relegation worries each season, it's bad enough for the players, it must be murder on the terraces. Blues must strengthen the team.**❞**

Trevor Francis, May 1976, after yet another battle against relegation

❛I enjoyed every minute of my career at St Andrews and if I had the chance I'd do it all over again. And I'd do it at Blues too!**❜**

Dave Latchford, Blues 'keeper 1966–1977

❛It was a great time to be manager of the Blues. Big crowds, big games and a great team. **❜**

Freddie Goodwin recalls managing Blues in the early 1970s

❝Bob Latchford said that I used to do all of his work and he used to score all of my goals.**❞**

Bob Hatton who was George Harrison to Trevor Francis's John Lennon and Bob Latchford's Paul McCartney in the famous Blues forward line of the 1970s

❝I didn't bother to take them normally because I didn't consider them to be a real goal.**❞**

Bob Latchford explains why he didn't take penalties

❝I was never fat, I was probably at my fattest, or heaviest, as I would prefer to call it, when I was younger, and I became slimmer with age.**❞**

Bob Latchford

"It's not all bad being an Evertonian: imagine if you supported Birmingham City, then you'd really have something to moan about."

Bob Latchford

> **❝**If it was there to be won, I would try to win it. In fact, even if it wasn't there, I'd still try.**❞**

Kenny Burns

❝He was the ultimate student of goalkeeping. To him, it was a geometric technique as well as an art which enabled him to be perpetually in the right place.**❞**

The Sports Argus *Birmingham City Centenary Souvenir* description of Gil Merrick, who played from 1946 to 1960 and was manager from 1960 to 1964, November 1975

❝Luck always looks the other way when Birmingham City are around.**❞**

Denis Shaw, *Sports Argus Birmingham City Centenary Souvenir*, November 1975

'Francis should have gone to Rome.'

Chant from aggrieved **Blues fans** after Trevor
Francis was left out of the England team by Don
Revie for a vital World Cup Qualifier in Italy in
November 1976. England lost the match 2–0 and
failed to qualify for the 1978 World Cup Finals. It
would be two more years before Francis finally
made his England debut

> ❝We will not sell him [Trevor Francis] at any price.❞

Chairman **Keith Coombs** makes a promise he cannot hope to keep, January 1978

❝Sir Alf Ramsey once told me that he thought I was better than Martin Peters, and we all know what Alf thought of him!**❞**

Kevin Dillon

❛No, I didn't hit him – he must have been tired.**❜**

Alberto Tarantino explains why Manchester United's Brian Greenhoff ended up on the deck next to him and was carried off during Blues' 5–1 thrashing of the Red Devils, November 1978

‘You lose some, you draw some.’

Jasper Carrott on being a Blues fan, 1979

❝ The supporters were so loyal to the club that the directors had it too easy. While the cash kept flowing in, they were never forced to go out and buy quality players. Whereas Nottingham Forest would spend £300,000 on Peter Shilton, Birmingham would try and buy half a team for that money. ❞

Trevor Francis, speaking shortly after his transfer to Nottingham Forest, 1979

❝Archie Gemmill has proved me wrong in a big way. It was a mistake to sell him to Birmingham. I let him go for £175,000 and I have spent almost £1m trying to replace him.**❞**

Brian Clough in the *Daily Express*, September 1980

❝You're going nowhere.❞

Manager **Ron Saunders** succinctly sums up
full-back Mark Dennis's career after selling him to
Southampton for a cut-price £30,000 in
November 1983

❝In two or three years David Seaman will be one of the top five goalkeepers in the country.❞

Ron Saunders appraises new signing David Seaman, October 1984

❝A couple of people had told me that [chairman] Ken Wheldon was so tight that on rainy days he switched off his windscreen wipers when he passed under railway bridges.❞

Dave Mackay, *The Dave Mackay Story*, 2004

❝ There is no noisier ground than Birmingham's when the team are in the throes of yet another promotion battle. **❞**

Simon Inglis, *The Football Grounds of Great Britain*, 1987

❝ St Andrews... a place of no fun, no players and no hope. **❞**

The Birmingham Evening Mail, January 1986

❛You wouldn't treat a dog the way I have been here.**❜**

John Bond after quitting as manager in 1987

❢This is the only job I ever wanted… I never dreamed of managing Liverpool or Manchester United, but I was prepared to walk barefoot across broken glass to be the manager of Birmingham City.**❣**

Garry Pendrey in his inaugural programme notes
for Blues versus Stoke City, August 15th 1987

❝I can see a little light at the end of what has been a very dark tunnel, hanks to the financial wizardry of the chairman, Ken Wheldon.❞

Garry Pendrey in the same programme notes

❝Q: How much money have you invested in Birmingham City, Mr Wheldon?

A: I don't propose to answer that.

Q: Why not?

A: I don't want to.**❞**

Exchange between chairman **Ken Wheldon** and **a frustrated shareholder** at Blues' Annual General Meeting, January 4th 1988

❝The agreement is 99% certain of being realised… it will make us one of the healthiest and wealthiest clubs in the land… it could be the most exciting thing that has ever happened at St Andrews.**❞**

Ken Wheldon makes empty promises to Blues shareholders about the sale of the club's training ground at the club's AGM, January 5th 1988

❝Supporters should be patient a little while longer – sunshine days are just around the corner.**❞**

A still hopeful **Ken Wheldon**, March 18th 1988

❝Birmingham City will be relegated over my dead body.**❞**

Ken Wheldon, autumn 1988

❝The day he bought Birmingham City, Ken Wheldon ripped the word "ambition" from its vocabulary.**❞**

Tired and Weary fanzine, Issue 6, April 1989

❝Birmingham City are not so much a sleeping giant, more comatose.**❞**

Central defender **Vince Overson**, 1989, who went on to captain Blues to the 1991 Leyland DAF Trophy

❝Q: Is there money still to spend on players?

A: I would defy anybody to make that guarantee – you have only got to look up the M6 at Manchester United to see that money doesn't necessarily buy success.❞

Samesh Kumar, *Sports Argus*, 24th February 1990

> While the reserves lost 6–1 at Stockport on Tuesday night, they still put up a very good performance.

Dave Mackay's programme notes, Blues v Rotherham, March 17th 1990, making many wonder precisely what would constitute a bad performance

❝I will always be known as the man who sold Britain's first £1m player – the supremely talented Trevor Francis. But the fact is, it never happened… Trevor moved to Forest for £1 short of the magic million mark. Peter Taylor said, "We don't want him to become big-headed so we aren't going to give you a million."❞

Jim Smith in his autobiography *Bald Eagle, The Jim Smith Story*, 1990

❛Another player I signed was Frank Worthington. I met Frank to discuss the deal and we quickly came to an agreement and drank and chatted through the night. I recall driving along the M6 next day thinking, "Christ, I've just signed a bloke who drank more whisky than me last night!"❜

Jim Smith

❝In my first game as manager, we were leading Newcastle 1–0 but conceded a late equaliser through someone not doing their job. I stormed into the dressing room and shouted, "That's useless!" plus a few choice expletives and smashed all the cups to the floor. But I knew what I was doing – they were all plastic!❞

Jim Smith

 ❝My debut for Blues was one of those games that everyone remembers. We raced into a 3–0 lead but ended up losing 4–3. As you might imagine, Jim Smith needed to order some more crockery the following day.**❞**

Tony Evans, who was a forward with Blues from 1979 to 1983

❝When I first arrived at Birmingham I stayed at the home of Chairman Keith Coombs, arriving in darkness. Next morning I went downstairs and said, "What a fabulous house – and what a fabulous view of the park." It wasn't the park... it was his garden.❞

Jim Smith

‘ Many years ago, the gypsies cursed St Andrews and Keith Coombs took it seriously enough to look for an exorcist. We ended up with the Greek Orthodox Church. Their priest turned out, complete with holy water and a cross. They even buried four crosses at each corner of the pitch! **’**

Jim Smith

❝Established names such as Dennis Bailey and Simon Sturridge equally fell victim to Dave Mackay's selection policy as they were shunted in and out and about the team like a drunken managerial version of the Hokey Cokey.❞

Jim Bryant, founder of *Tired and Weary* fanzine, about Blues' newly departed manager Dave Mackay, April 1991

"When people tell me that fans want style and entertainment first I don't believe it. Fans want to win trophies, style's a bonus."

Lou Macari on his tactics as boss of Birmingham City in *The Wit and Wisdom of Football*

❝If that man's a donkey, get off to Blackpool beach and sign another six.**❞**

Blues fan after much-criticised striker John Gayle's spectacular overhead kick won Blues the 1991 Leyland DAF Cup Final versus Tranmere, May 1991

❝ I am only interested in staying at a
football club that is prepared to let
me have a team for the future – if
that's not the case, I will be off. **❞**

Manager **Lou Macari**, speaking immediately after
Blues' victory in the Leyland DAF Cup Final,
May 27th 1991

"He was a man of few words, and most of them were "No". "

Line from Blues fanzine *Tired and Weary's* obituary of former Chairman Ken Wheldon

‘Stay at home in future – you don't want to see this at a football match.’

Terry Cooper's despondent remark to a six-year-old fan after rioting marred Blues' home game with Stoke, February 29th 1992

❛Why have I bought Birmingham City? Because football is good for society.**❜**

David Sullivan, 1993

Q: What attracted you to Birmingham City?

A: Nothing, I was told by my boss to come here.

Karren Brady in an interview with the fanzine of Kings Heath Concorde FC

❛Well, that's us through to the next round.**❜**

David Sullivan on hearing Blues had drawn Kidderminster Harriers at home in the FA Cup 3rd Round, December 1993, from Barry Fry's autobiography *Big Fry*

❝If I was the Kidderminster boss,
I would fancy my chances.**❞**

Barry Fry, prior to Blues versus Kidderminster FA
Cup 3rd Round tie which Blues lost 2–1,
January 1994

❝The 1980s was the era of the Yuppie, of Loadsamoney. For Blues, it was the era of the Floppie, the decade of decay, football losers on and off the pitch, with no money.**❞**

Colin Tattum, *Birmingham Evening Mail, History of the Blues supplement*, January 24th 1994

❝Why?❞

Banner carried around the pitch by fans at the
last home game against Bristol City before the
demolition of Spion Kop and the Tilton Road
terracing, April 16th 1994

"Even if you are the worst manager in the world, you should at least win once in three months!**"**

Barry Fry, *The Encyclopedia of Birmingham City Football Club 1875–2000*

❝Q: Can Birmingham City become another Aston Villa, as it were?

A: I think we set our sights probably higher than that.**❞**

Karren Brady answers a question on
Sky TV, 1994

❝Footballers are only interested in drinking, clothes and the size of their willies. **❞**

Karren Brady, 1994

"I told the lads, "Let's stick it up Andy." They went out and did just that and it's nice to see a Scotsman part with his money."

Barry Fry after Blues' FA Cup First Round Replay victory at Scunthorpe cost Sky TV pundit Andy Gray a £5 bet, December 14th 1994

❝We concentrated instead on Birmingham's battle with relegation and, when the news filtered through that they had finally gone down, I smoked my first-ever cigar in the centre of the Roots Hall pitch.❞

Roots Hall Roar fanzine savours revenge on the club who poached their manager Barry Fry, January 1995

❝Barry Fry's Birmingham City gave us a hell of a game which ended in a penalty shoot-out. The Brummies then decided that they didn't like someone in the crowd and proceeded to use their spot kicks to hit him.❞

Liverpool's **All Day and All of the Night** fanzine,
January 1995

  ❝We [the directors] are not going to sit around meekly while our money goes up the wall. If we published our views about the way we've played this season, we'd have to sell the official programme off the top shelf at newsagents.**❞**

Karren Brady discusses the start of the 1994–95 season, *Brady Plays the Blues*

❛My first emotions on seeing St Andrews were not so much disappointment as disgust. I remember walking out on to the pitch and feeling I had stepped into a time warp. You could wipe a finger down a wall and inspect five generations of filthy dust. It was hard to tell the broom cupboards from the boardroom.**❜**

Karren Brady

❝I was chatting away when this man came up to me and introduced himself as the linesman; "I gave that goal to your side and everyone says it's offside." "Don't worry about it," I told him. "I'm not," he replied, "I'm retiring today." "Get this man a drink," we shouted. The celebrations went on until four in the morning.❞

Karren Brady after Paul Moulden's winner against Charlton kept Blues in the Second Division at the end of the 1992–93 season, *Brady Plays the Blues*

I told David Sullivan: "The press are following me, I've done something you might be a bit angry with." "Don't worry," he said, "nothing can be that bad – it's not as if you've run off with one of the footballers." "Well, actually, I have – it's Paul Peschisolido." "Thank God for that," he replied, "at least it's not one of Villa's."

Karren Brady

> **❝**Most clubs in our Division can't get in the newspapers; we can't get out of them.**❞**

Karren Brady, *Brady Plays the Blues*

❝When I first visited Barry's training ground I was horrified. Some players wore red, some wore black, some wore blue; there was even one bloke training in an overcoat. I left with my head spinning, it looked so amateurish.❞

Karren Brady

‟We are honest and sensible enough to know that spending money in the transfer market does not always guarantee success. No, money just increases your chances from nil to possible.„

Karren Brady, *Brady Plays the Blues*

❝I remember when I was at school and we used to play twenty-a-side with two captains. Whoever got to pick first ended up with the best team and won most times. That's what we have got in this division because we have got more money than any other team – we pick first.❞

David Sullivan, *The Heathen* fanzine, 1995

'We have just bought the most awesome striker in this Division. Everyone is frightened of Kevin Francis. '

David Sullivan, *The Heathen fanzine*, 1995

‘Jose Dominguez – I love him. He's good on soft pitches and hard pitches. He can destroy defences – I like to see him brought on when defenders have got yellow cards!**’**

David Sullivan, *The Heathen* fanzine, 1995

"What do you see in the future for Blues?"

"It's easy to say it, but you've got to talk about David Sullivan and the Golds. They are not going to be satisfied until we're in the Premier League – that's their ambition. Providing we're getting the support, they won't rest until we make it."

Blues Director **Jack Wiseman**,
The Heathen fanzine, 1995

❝It would be great to win promotion, it would be great to win at Wembley, but what would top it all is to beat Villa in Paul McGrath's Testimonial. What a season that would be!❞

Lifelong Blues fan and 6ft7in centre-forward **Kevin Francis**, Auto Windscreens Shield Final match programme, 1995

❛He's a great tactician, which is something I admire because I don't do tactics.**❜**

Barry Fry on Terry Venables, 1995

"If a jumbo jet was coming towards our area, he'd try to head it clear."

Barry Fry on Liam Daish, 1995

❝If left to their own devices players would have two weeks in Tenerife, another two in Cyprus and two more in the pub.❞

David Sullivan on allegations that Blues' 1995 pre-season training was too gruelling

❝He doesn't know a goal line from a clothes line.**❞**

Barry Fry on Blues owner David Sullivan

❝ Jose? There ain't been anyone as exciting in this country since George Best. I love him, the crowd love him, everybody loves him. But when you analyse it, his final ball is ****. Full stop. **❞**

Barry Fry on Jose Dominguez

❝I can understand the fans chanting, "Fry Out". In fact, the chants were led by my dad.**❞**

Barry Fry contemplating a run of bad results

❝ Q: If you won the National Lottery, what would you buy?

A: 25 strikers. **❞**

Barry Fry, Blues match programme,
Q&A Section, 1996

❝ I've told the players not to worry about me if I get sacked. I'll walk out that door into three other jobs – at Stourbridge, Nuneaton or Atherstone! **❞**

Barry Fry shortly before his dismissal in 1996

❝I tried to come here and use an attacking system I've used for the last twenty-five years. Even a blind man can see it was completely wrong.**❞**

Barry Fry, 1996

' His management style seems to be based on the chaos theory. **,**

Mark McGhee, Wolves manager on
Barry Fry, 1996

❝ You took your kit home to make sure you'd got one the next day. We'd know there were five or six trialists coming in. **❞**

Ian Bennett describes the chaotic reign of Barry Fry

❝ He was the walking, waddling *Who's Who* of the underbelly of the English game. **❞**

Ian Ridley on Barry Fry,
Tales From The Boot Camps

❝I remember one time he was having a go at our midfielder Paul Tait, calling him a skinny bastard. Taity came back with, "You fat bastard". They were standing there face to face for about five minutes, one shouting, "You skinny bastard", the other shouting, "You fat bastard."❞

Gary Poole remembers the sheer quality of Barry Fry's conversational prowess, *Tales From The Boot Camps*

‘Someone said you could write Barry's knowledge of tactics on a stamp. You'd need to fold the stamp in half.’

Steve Claridge, 1997,
Tales From The Boot Camps

❝ People will think I'm crackers.
I'm voluntarily going back to
the madhouse. **❞**

Trevor Francis on returning to
Blues as manager, May 1996

Our fans would find something to moan about if we signed Alan Shearer.

David Sullivan, after Blues sold just 25 season tickets in 72 hours following the club's first £1m signing, Paul Furlong, in 1996

"We were the original "Crazy Gang" – a bunch of young guys thrown into the first team because of the financial situation. We lacked a few experienced heads in the dressing room. Certain things we got up to off the pitch, there's no way we should have done them. You wouldn't get away with that now."

Noel Blake, *Match of the Day* magazine, February 1998

He was tougher than me, he used to scare opponents to death. When we had chicken for our pre-match meals, Noel would eat the bones too.

Mick Harford on Noel Blake, *MOTD magazine*, February 1998

❝It's no good turning up five minutes before kick-off. I want the Watford players to be put under pressure from 7:15pm when they come out to warm up.❞

Manager **Trevor Francis** urges a white-hot St Andrews atmosphere for the 1999 First Division Play-Off Semi-Final Second Leg which ended 4–1 aet (agg. 4–2)

❛Jim Smith is one of the best managers the recent game has known. If the board had only been a little more patient, the quality players he brought together would surely have taken the club to the summit that they and their fans deserve.**❜**

Frank Worthington, *125 Years of Birmingham City commemorative brochure*, 2000

❝I think it's true to say I'm the steadying influence. David is a very emotional character, and says it as i is, and Karren is forthright. We've a got egos but sometimes some of them need to be massaged and that's what I do very well.**❞**

David Gold, *MOTD magazine,* November 2000

❝I said after our semi-final defeat of Ipswich Town that had I not been in the dugout I would have been in the stands cheering the boys on. That's what I feel about this club… it has a special place in my heart.❞

Trevor Francis before Blues' League Cup Final appearance against Liverpool, February 2001

> **❝**This was joyfully, gloriously Blues' Night of Nights. Never in their trophy-challenged history has there been one like it.**❞**

The Birmingham Evening Mail, February 1st 2001, on Blues' League Cup Semi-Final victory over Ipswich Town

‛When Trevor first appeared as a 16-year old it was clear from the start that he had special talent. People talk about Michael Owen when he came through, but I reckon Trevor was way in front, even of Michael. On the technical side he was simply sensational. ,

Bob Latchford League Cup Final match programme, February, 2001

‘ He hugged me, I hugged him. He was close to tears and so was I. We both had this empty feeling and we just kind of tried to comfort each other. **'**

Andrew Johnson sought solace with manager Trevor Francis after his missed penalty led to defeat in the 2001 Worthington Cup Final, February 25th 2001

❝ Go from here and get ready
for the Premiership. **❞**

Chairman **David Gold**'s presidential message
to Blues fans at the League Cup Final
Civic Reception, February 2001

「 "You couldn't buy this excitement," proclaimed Alan Parry on the telly highlights I watched later. Well, you could, Alan, and it cost me fifty quid. What a bargain. **」**

Tim Stainthorpe, Blues programme columnist, recalls the drama of Blues injury-time equaliser against Liverpool at Cardiff, Blues v Watford match programme, March 2001

❛We don't welcome yobs in any form, but that isn't to say we're against tribal loyalty. And our tribe aren't half fearsome when they want something.**❜**

Karren Brady, 2002

The most important match in the club's history.

Steve Bruce's view of the First Division Play-Off Final against Norwich City, *Birmingham Evening Mail*, May 2002

❝If Stern John becomes any more laid-back, he'll fall asleep standing up.**❞**

Steve Bruce, First Division Play-Off Final match programme, May 2002

❝ I can't remember anything about the move really other than that I headed it and it went over the line. I was going to go in with my feet but I misjudged it. **❞**

Geoff Horsfield recalls his equalising goal in Blues' First Division Play-Off Final victory over Norwich City, Cardiff, May 12th 2002

❝ I said if I scored was it all over? and the ref replied, "Yes." **❞**

Darren Carter, before his penalty against Norwich won the First Division Play-Off Final, Cardiff, May 12th 2002

❝Dad, I'm in heaven with you.**❞**

Banner, raised by Blues supporter after Blues'
First Division Play-Off Final victory over Norwich
City, Cardiff, May 12th 2002

❝This is a fantastic achievement. Our supporters sing about keeping right on to the end of the road – we have finally reached the end of that road.❞

Karren Brady following Blues' Play-Off victory, *Birmingham Evening Mail*, May 13th 2002

❝ I am in a state of euphoria. I cannot wait for all the big games we get, especially Villa – they've had it easy for too long. **❞**

Blues Chairman **David Gold** following promotion victory, *Birmingham Evening Mail*, May 13th 2002

'It feels unbelievable. I've done some things in my life but this achievement has just beaten anything I've ever done.'

David Gold

❝ When Trevor Francis left I received an astounding amount of abuse, but all the changes we made were for the benefit of the club. If we hadn't made them, we wouldn't have been in the play-offs, let alone the Premier League. ❞

David Sullivan, *Birmingham Evening Mail*,
May 13th 2002

When I used to watch Roy Rogers on his white horse, Trigger, he never lost. He always won because he was the good guy. The bloke on the black horse with the mask; the baddie who killed, raped and pillaged, always got beat. I want that to continue here.

David Gold, 2002

I'd kick my dad if it meant winning that's just the way it is.

Robbie Savage, *Birmingham Evening Mail*
football annual, August 2002

❝ If you throw it to your 'keeper, you're not expecting him to miss it. **❞**

Graham Taylor on Peter Enckelman's own goal in Blues 3–0 victory over Villa, September 2002

❝He said he didn't know any of our players – that fired us up. We pinned his comments up in the dressing room.**❞**

Robbie Savage on Aston Villa captain Olof Mellberg, September 2002

"I was jumping around screaming, "Yes!" when my wife told me that our pet parrot Charlie had collapsed in his cage. The shock of my scream was too much for his heart... he hadn't been very well lately."

Tom Roberts, Druids Heath on hearing news of Blues' first Premiership goal, *Brum's The Word*

❝I haven't been so excited since I hit the floating planet to win a speed boat on *The Golden Shot* in 1974.❞

Blues fan after 3–0 win over Aston Villa,
Brum's The Word

If this is heaven, roll on death.

Blues fan, *Brum's The Word*

❛Steve Bruce told me that the club wouldn't sell me for love nor money. That was nice to hear and the matter is now over and I am looking forward to a long career with Birmingham City and hopefully enjoying some success here. **❜**

Robbie Savage, *Blues Magazine*,
November 2003

❝Mark Dennis was my hero – I loved him. I thought he was superb, not because of his wild side – although that did help.❞

Julian Dicks

❛All I ever wanted to do was play football. I had no intentions of doing school work, or anything like that, I had my mind set on being a professional footballer.**❜**

Julian Dicks, *Blues Magazine*, November 2003

❝It looked as if we'd picked eleven people off the streets of Birmingham and asked them if they wanted a game.**❞**

Steve Bruce, Blues versus Sunderland, *Daily Telegraph*, February 26th 2004

❝ I know it's not very PC, but it's not the crime of the decade. It's been blown out of all proportion. I heard absolutely nothing. **❞**

David Sullivan on the racial abuse aimed at Dwight Yorke at Ewood Park, *The Birmingham Post*, November 23rd 2004

❝ There were two or three people at one end of the ground who were giving him a bit of abuse, but he could have run to the other end. **❞**

David Sullivan

❝ I'd just like to dedicate this performance to Ollie Mellborg. **❞**

Robbie Savage in typically magnanimous mood following Blues 2–1 victory at Villa Park, BBC Radio WM, 12th December 2004, after Mellborg had said he didn't like BCFC and didn't know anyone who played for them

❝Blackburn faxed me an offer for Robbie which was a waste of fax paper and a waste of my time reading it.❞

Karren Brady, December 22nd 2004

❝No one should ever doubt my commitment to Birmingham City.**❞**

Robbie Savage, Blues v Middlesbrough
matchday programme, December 26th 2004,
shortly before demanding a move to Blackburn
during the transfer window